A BOOK IN THE **EXPLAINS SERIES**

MODEL RAILWAYS is published
by
The Haynes Publishing Group of Sparkford, Yeovil, Somerset, BA22 7JJ,
England

© The Haynes Publishing Group 1977
First published October 1977

ISBN 0 85429 546 1

Printed and bound in Great Britain
Cover photograph P. Godfrey 'Heckmondwike (Midland)' station on the
North London Group's Scale Four layout
Editor Tim Parker
Layout Annette Cutler

1

INTRODUCTION

Why do people make model railways? The answer is very simple; as a modelling acquaintance of the author once said, we do it because we like doing it. But if you then ask why we like doing it, the answer is more complex; there are a great many kinds of model railways and almost as many reasons for building them.

Railway modelling is, in fact, not just 'playing trains' but a satisfying and challenging adult hobby. Little Johnny, with his plastic 'Jinty' circumnavigating its oval of track on the carpet at jet-fighter speed, is indeed, 'playing trains'; but once he adds a turnout or two and some rudimentary buildings, he is taking the first step into real modelling — a hobby which may, half a lifetime later, see him building models whose background research is genuine industrial archaeology and whose execution is a true art form in four dimensions. (Four, because to the three dimensions of the static model is added that of time when the layout is in operation).

For many of us there is an element of nostalgia in railway modelling. Stepping out of a Great Western or Southern branch train into country-scented air had something special about it which is missing from our present 'holidays' as harassed chauffeurs; something that we can partly recapture by building a working model of that branch train and its station. Many of us, our lives controlled by those higher up the pecking order, long for a situation in which **we** are in command and make the decisions; we find this in the design and organisation of a little empire of our own. Others, with the well-known certainty of the middle-aged that things were a lot better when they were young, re-create a corner of the world of their youth to which they can turn for spiritual refreshment.

Some builders take a more technological viewpoint. A great many model railways are based on ideas of what a railway might have been; some start by assuming that an actual railway company built a line to a place, either fictitious or real but without a rail connection, and design its operation in just the same way as its full-size entrepreneurs would have done. Others make the line entirely freelance, starting only with a situation and

'Firing up' at a Gauge 1 garden meeting

designing line, rolling stock and motive power to suit it. Yet others find great satisfaction in recording as faithfully as possible — often with a great deal of historical research — the style and activities of a particular railway company that catches their interest. Some are fascinated by the elegance, beauty and fitness for purpose displayed by old railway vehicles as in the best antiques; at the other end of the scale some like to use a model railway as a research tool in pursuing lines of development abandoned by the full-size railways.

None of these reasons, however, can explain the universal appeal of model railways; certainly nostalgia alone cannot account for the many excellent models being built by people too young to have ever travelled behind their prototype, or even seen a steam loco in main-line service. To my mind, the reason may lie in an instinctive respect, conscious or not, for the engineers who built the first railways. Inventing is easy nowadays because there is such a huge background of technical knowhow to draw on; but those pioneers were breaking entirely new ground. The jump from the stationary steam engine to the 'Rocket' was bigger than that from the 'Rocket' to the UP 'Big Boy'. From these beginnings the railway spread to become something that touched, and in most cases enriched, the lives of almost everyone in this country. Not long ago I made my first trip in a 125mph HST along a line that was laid out over a century ago when the fastest conveyance was a good horse. Before that kind of foresight and imagination, one can only show the deepest respect; I like to think that our models are all, in some way, expressions of that respect, whether we realise it or not.

All this sounds terribly pompous, and we must not forget that the idea of a hobby is to give enjoyment and relaxation. At its highest level, the building of railway models demands from its devotees the skills of engineer, artist and manager combined, and will continue to extend and enhance those skills for as long as they pursue the hobby. But the nice thing about railway modelling is its flexibility; if you prefer to concentrate on operation of a model assembled entirely from off-the-shelf items, you are no less a railway modeller than the chap who chooses to spend a lifetime building a Beyer-Garratt complete to the last rivet. In its way, modelling is an allegory of the railway itself. You can go all the way to a number of interesting destinations, you can get off at any point along the journey, or go on or back — or even take a cross-country connection to a line leading somewhere else. No other hobby that I can think of offers such adaptability to the abilities and needs of those who take it up.

The reader of this book will find little information about commercially available equipment. To some extent this is due to my personal preference for building models rather than buying them; but apart from the fact that the model market changes so rapidly that including such information would guarantee the book's being out of date almost as soon as it was printed, it can easily be obtained, in more up-to-date form, from catalogues or over the counter of a model shop. What, to my mind, is more important in a basic book such as this is to get the basic principles across so that, armed with this information, the reader can make up his own mind about the kind of railway he wants and the way to achieve it.

(Left) Although constrained by quite a small room and using a large proportion of commercial models, John Crooke's 'Weymouth' captures the atmosphere of a busy seaside terminus in the era of steam

(Below) An outstanding example of the modeller's art: 'King George V' in 4mm scale by Guy Williams (P. Williams)

8

Man is a gregarious creature, and the railway modeller is seldom an exception. Most large towns have a model railway club; for those out of reach of one, there are several societies dealing with particular scales and interests, conducting most of their business by post or on the basis of local meetings. In addition there are three model railway magazines published monthly which contain a lot of useful information. Learning can be a slow process if you have to make all the mistakes personally; contact with kindred spirits through these channels can save you a lot of trial and error and enhance the enjoyment. Cultivate an open mind, tempered with enough suspicion to distinguish the voice of experience from that of prejudice; listen to everyone except those who tell you that 'such-and-such is impossible'. It seldom is.

This seems a good moment to thank all those modellers whose brains I have picked over the years. It is a real pleasure to be able to pass on some of the information they so willingly gave me.

GAUGES, SCALES AND STANDARDS

Gauge and **scale** are two very important terms in model railways, and are often confused; it is necessary to understand clearly what they mean. **Gauge** is the distance between the inner faces of the running rails, while **scale** is the ratio or fraction relating a dimension on the prototype to its equivalent on the model. Between them, gauge and scale govern the size of a model. You might, indeed, think that it was only necessary to express one (assuming that the gauge of the prototype was known) for the other to be implied, but, as we shall see, this is not entirely true.

A third, almost equally important term is **standards**. Almost any old pair of wheels of the right gauge will run on plain track, but at pointwork the dimensions of the wheels and of the gaps in the rails have to be carefully matched so that the wheels can pass without jamming or jolting. It is possible to make a layout work just by persistent fiddling, adjusting wheels and points to fit each other, but for each of the commonly used gauges there is a set of dimensions laid down (see the table at the end of this chapter) and if all the wheels and all the points are made to these measurements the layout will work. Then if there is a derailment, it is easy, by using gauges, to decide whether the wheels or the track are at fault and to correct it.

Some people like to have everything on their railways as nearly exact to scale as possible, including the wheels and track; this is known as a **fine-scale** standard. Others think that, because model-railway curves have to be much sharper than scale and because it is difficult to get the track proportionally as accurate as the prototype, the wheel flanges should be deeper and thicker and the rail gaps correspondingly larger; this is known as a **coarse-scale** or commercial standard.

British engines are usually smaller than Continental or American ones. Thus, when the first 'table-top' railways came here from Germany, it was thought impossible to get a motor into a British model of the same scale, and one solution was to use a slightly larger **scale** for the bodywork without altering the **gauge.** This was first done in 00 and has been repeated each time a smaller scale has been commercially introduced here, even though it is now unnecessary. So for some gauges there are several scales, or for some scales several different gauges, and for each combination there may be several standards. Models of different scales can run together, though they usually look rather silly doing so, but mixing of gauges and wheel standards is never a success. So, before starting the layout, you have to choose a standard — and stick to it.

Gauge 1, 45mm between rails, was once thought to be the smallest gauge for a model railway. The commonest scale is 10mm to the foot, but some builders prefer 3/8in to the foot (1/32) as it is more nearly correct for the track gauge and makes scaling easier. Gauge 1 rolling stock is big and heavy enough to suggest the massiveness of full-size trains, and appeals to the modeller who likes to experiment with scale springing and steam locomotives; but it is too big for all but the biggest houses and even for an average-sized garden, and has to be all handbuilt — and even then is expensive.

Gauge 0, 32mm between rails with a scale of 7mm/ft, shares some of the advantages of Gauge 1 but will fit into a suburban garden or, with some cramming, a large loft. Some readymade equipment is available, but is still expensive because it is made in relatively small quantities.

HO (half 0) has a gauge of 16.5mm and a scale of 3.5mm/ft (1/87) though some makers use a slightly larger scale. It is standard on the Continent and in America; attempts to introduce models of British prototypes have not been very successful, but many British modellers run layouts based on American or European practice in this scale.

00 gauge is by far the most popular in Britain. The gauge is the same as HO — 16.5mm — but the scale is enlarged to 4mm/ft (1.76). A very wide range of ready-made models and kits are available in this scale, fairly cheap because of the quantities in which they are made; not all firms use the same wheel standards. The scale is equally suitable for building from scratch.

Some of the best 4mm scale kits, fitted with scale wheels and carefully painted, are almost impossible to tell from the real thing in a photograph. Many modellers feel that this excellence should not be spoilt by an incorrect track gauge. EM gauge (18mm between rails) gives a much better appearance but is still fairly tolerant of sharp curves; most kits and ready-to-run models can easily be converted to it by replacing the wheels. Recently it has been proved that, given good workmanship, exact-scale wheels and track can work in 4mm scale; there are two such standards, Scalefour and Protofour, each with its own society and differing slightly in the method of laying out dimensions and tolerances.

TT — 12mm gauge — has almost died out abroad but has a faithful following in Britain where the scale is 3mm/ft. The commercial (Triang) standard is very coarse, but there is a finer one for general use, and an exact-scale standard has been shown to be practicable. No ready-made equipment is now available, but the 3mm Society regularly sponsors the production of kits and parts for members. TT is an attractive scale, taking up less room than 00 but still large enough for the construction of detailed models.

N gauge measures 9mm between rails. Most of the technical

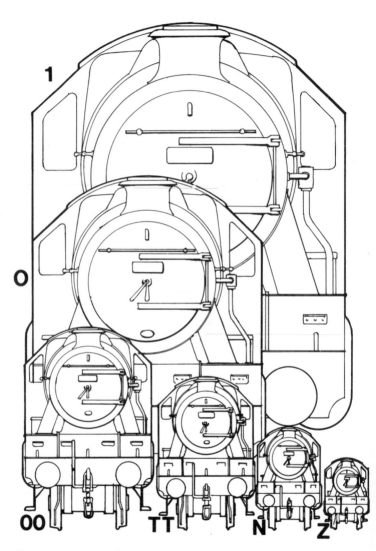

1

O

00

TT

N

Z

Comparison of scales (actual size)

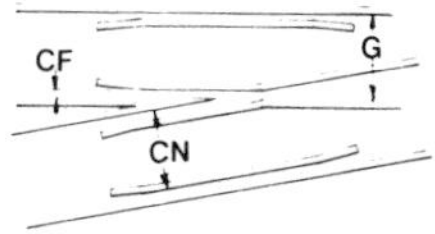

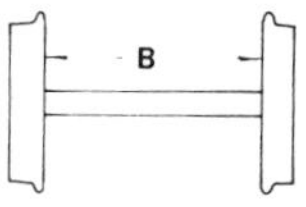

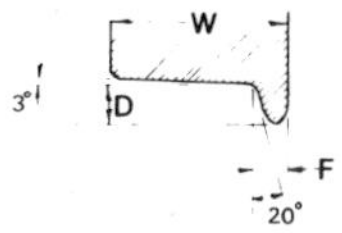

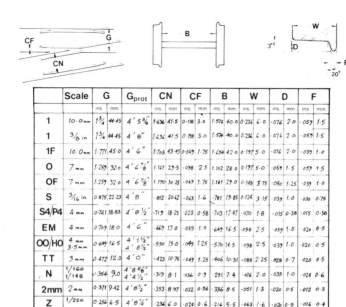

	Scale	G		G_{prot}	CN		CF		B		W		D		F	
		ins	mm		ins.	mm	ins.	mm	ins	mm	ins.	mm	ins.	mm.	ins.	mm.
1	10.0mm	1¾	44.45	4′ 5⅜″	1.636	41.5	0.118	3.0	1.574	40.0	0.236	6.0	.076	2.0	.059	1.5
1	⅜ in	1¾	44.45	4′ 8″	1.636	41.5	0.118	3.0	1.574	40.0	0.236	6.0	.076	2.0	.059	1.5
1F	10.0mm	1.771	45.0	4′ 6″	1.703	43.45	0.069	1.75	1.654	42.0	0.197	5.0	.076	2.0	.039	1.0
O	7mm	1.259	32.0	4′ 6⅞″	1.161	29.5	.098	2.5	1.102	28.0	0.197	5.0	.059	1.5	.059	1.5
OF	7mm	1.259	32.0	4′ 6⅞″	1.190	30.25	.069	1.75	1.141	29.0	0.148	3.75	.050	1.25	.039	1.0
S	3/16 in	0.875	22.23	4′ 8″	.812	20.62	.063	1.6	.781	19.85	0.124	3.15	.039	1.0	.030	0.75
S4/P4	4mm	0.741	18.83	4′ 8½″	.719	18.25	.023	0.58	.703	17.87	.070	1.8	.015	0.38	.015	0.38
EM	4mm	0.709	18.0	4′ 6″	.669	17.0	.039	1.0	.649	16.5	.098	2.5	.039	1.0	.020	0.5
OO/HO	4mm 3.5mm	0.649	16.5	4′ 1½″ 4′ 8½″	.590	15.0	.049	1.25	.570	14.5	.098	2.5	.039	1.0	.020	0.5
TT	3mm	0.472	12.0	4′ 0″	.423	10.75	.049	1.25	.406	10.31	.088	2.25	.028	0.7	.020	0.5
N	1/160 1/148	0.354	9.0	4′ 8⅝″ 4′ 4½″	.319	8.1	.036	0.9	.291	7.4	.076	2.0	.039	1.0	.024	0.6
2mm	2mm	0.371	9.42	4′ 8½″	.353	8.97	.022	0.56	.336	8.5	.051	1.3	.020	0.5	.012	0.3
Z	1/220	0.256	6.5	4′ 8¼″	.236	6.0	.024	0.6	.216	5.5	.063	1.6	.020	0.5	.016	0.4

Standards for the common modelling scales

This table gives only the leading dimensions for each of the scale/gauge combination commonly used in this country. The column Gprot shows the model gauge scaled up to full size and so indicates the extent to which it differs from the true scale reduction of 4ft 8½in.

As far as possible the figures given are those recommended by the BRMSB, or where no recommendation has been made, those used by the appropriate society. Most of the dimensions are subject to a tolerance and full details can be obtained from the society in question. In general, all dimensions except B and F should be regarded as minimum values. B is a 'nominal' figure which should be adhered to as closely as possible; F, the effective flange width, is measured in a variety of ways but will usually have been taken care of when ready-made wheels are used.

The ends of check and wing rails should be bent outwards to give a gap equal to 1¾/2 times CF at the entry, the 'flare' being a scale 2ft 6 in.

Wheel profiles are specified in different ways in each scale, but most contain the essential features of a substantial radius where the flange meets the tread, a tread coned at approximately 3°, a taper of some 20° on the outer face of the flange, well-rounded edges to the flange and a small 45° chamfer at the outer edge of the tread.

No official figures for Z gauge are available at present; the figures given are based on measurements of commercial equipment problems of making such small models commercially have been overcome, and the best Continental and American models, to a scale of 1/160, are very accurate and splendidly detailed, though expensive. British models, 'officially' to the larger scale of 1/148, are mostly less realistic, and the range of models available is limited. The fine-scale equivalent of N is 2mm/ft scale; in this scale nearly everything has to be hand-built, but again there is an active Association which can supply basic parts and a few kits.

The latest in small gauges is Z, 6.5mm gauge with a scale of 1/220. At present only one maker, Märklin, produces it; although well made, the models are very expensive, and only a small range of Continental prototypes are modelled.

Some modellers like to model a narrow-gauge prototype, and several combinations of established scales and gauges conveniently fit the commoner narrow gauges; thus 2mm scale on Z gauge track approximates to metre gauge, 4mm on N gauge to 2ft 3in, and so on. Track and wheels from the smaller scale can be combined with scenic accessories and modified rolling-stock parts from the larger, to give a convincing result. Track and wheel standards usually follow the coarse-scale standard for the track gauge.

Coarse-scale equipment is more tolerant of uneven baseboards and lets you assemble a layout quickly from ready-made items; it is thus favoured for layouts where the chief interest is operating. A fine-scale layout takes longer to finish, because everything has to be hand-built, kit-built or converted; but when complete it looks far better and runs more smoothly. If you like making things and have the patience to wait a little while to get something running, fine scale will be more satisfying; do not be put off by doubts about your workmanship, because your skill will quickly improve with practice.

To decide whether you can cope with a chosen scale — try it. Build a couple of wagons, a turnout and a few yards of track. The cost will be minimal, but the exercise will tell whether the scale and you suit each other.

WHAT SORT OF A LAYOUT — AND WHERE?

In designing a layout, it is necessary to find a compromise between what you want from it and the available space. One person may see himself as the Superintendent of a busy station; another, more interested in loco-building, may need only an oval test track with little or no scenery, while a third may want to be a 'lineside watcher', observing a succession of trains passing through a country station or along a main line. Other questions to be settled include: is the layout to be taken to exhibitions? Does it represent a branch or main line? How many operators will be available?

Space is always a problem; no modeller ever admits to having enough. A full-size railway is a very big thing; a train of locomotive and ten coaches in 4mm scale is nearly ten feet long, more than the length of some layout-rooms. This can be solved by using a smaller scale; by modelling a smaller prototype, eg; a branch line where three-coach trains are normal; by finding more space, in the loft or the garden; or by 'selective compression', which is an imposing name for running short trains short distances between short stations and using one's imagination to supply the rest. Most layouts rely on this to some degree.

One way of finding enough space is to build the layout in the garden, and if the two are planned and developed together they enhance each other in a very satisfying way. On the other hand, it is not much fun running a railway in pouring rain, and the track and other fixed items must be made weatherproof and strong enough to resist damage by birds, cats, and so on, which implies a large scale and may cancel out the advantage of the larger space. Some modellers keep the exterior track very simple and locate the main station in a shed to protect the pointwork and buildings from weather and wildlife. Successful garden layouts have been built in 00 and even N gauge.

A dry and clean garage is a possible site for a layout, the car being parked outside while running goes on. Most modern saloon cars are only about 4ft 6in tall and the baseboards can be arranged to clear the roof by an inch or two, bringing the railway conveniently near the eye-level of a standing operator. Damp is

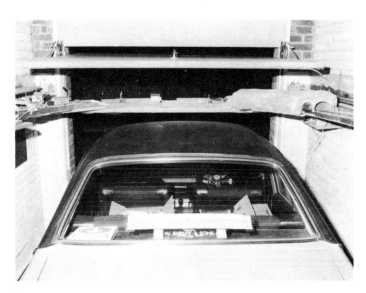

A layout in a garage *(J. F. W. Paige)*

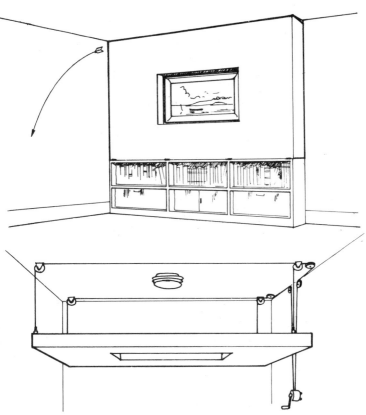

Wall and ceiling stowage for indoor layouts

the chief problem; a car brought in out of the rain releases a lot of moisture into the air as it dries.

The loft is a popular site, being usually the largest indoor space any house offers. Here the problem will be variations in temperature; the cure is to line the **roof** with insulating board, rather than insulating at ceiling level. (This will also help to keep the water tank from freezing). The floor will have to be boarded in, at least in the operating areas; check that the rafters are strong enough to carry the weight of the operator and any guests.

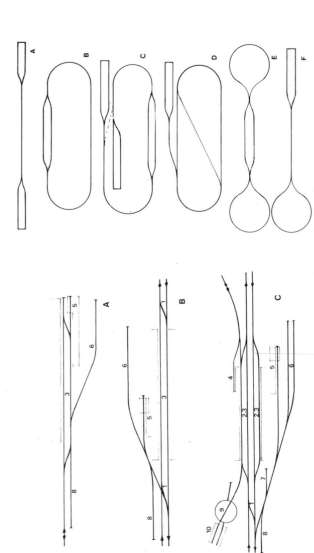

Types of layout: A, end to end; B, continuous run with station or fiddle-yard: C, two terminal with intermediate fiddle yard and optional continuous-run link: D, continuous run with terminus and return loop: E, dogbone; F, half-dog-bone with terminus

Typical station layout: A, small single-track branch terminus; B, passing station on double track main line: C, medium-sized junction. The numbers refer to the features listed in the text

If a big enough spare room is available for the layout, it can be built there more or less permanently; but often the layout-room has to double as a bedroom or living-room. The railway can be built as a series of sections which are stacked or stood on end, in a corner or alcove, and brought out and bolted together for running. This form of construction is useful anyway if the layout is to be taken to exhibitions or if one moves house often. Other possible ways of fitting a layout include hingeing it to the wall or hoisting it flush against the ceiling by ropes and pulleys; the underside in each case being boxed in and papered or painted to match the room decor in the 'stowed' position.

Layouts can be broadly divided into 'end to end' and 'continuous run' types. Real railways always run from somewhere to somewhere else, but the distances involved are much too great to be reproduced in full. We can get over this in several ways:

1 By representing one terminal station only and concentrating on the activities there, the rest of the railway being represented by a group of storage sidings or 'fiddle yard' hidden from the main layout by a scenic barrier.

2 By representing the two termini and interposing a double-ended 'fiddle yard' where trains may be held to represent their journey along the main line.

3 By providing a continuous loop of main line around which trains can run for as many laps as are needed to make up the desired duration of run. Two termini can be arranged on spurs from the loop, or a 'return loop' can be used to reverse the trains' direction so that it starts from, and returns to, a single terminal station.

4 By modelling only a part of the main line, perhaps including a through station, as a continuous loop part of which is a 'fiddle yard'.

A continuous loop can be squeezed in the middle to give the effect of double track over most of the distance; this is known as a 'dogbone' loop. Similarly one can have a 'half dogbone' where the apparent double track ends in a terminus. The loop or loops can be hidden under hills and placed one above the other to save space; the double-track section can itself be folded one or more times to give a longer run.

Station workings, especially at termini and junctions, are more interesting as trains are split up, made up or reversed, engines changed and serviced, and so on; but a continuous run, or a section of main line supposedly several miles from a main station, is the only realistic setting for a train travelling at full speed. A continuous loop is also useful for 'running in' new or overhauled locomotives, and some 'end-to-end' layouts incorporate a link (eg; an 'industrial siding' which disappears behind a wall and returns to the fiddle yard) to give this facility.

This discussion presupposes that the railway is electric. Other motive power limits the distance between stations; clockwork needs to be wound and steam locos need their fires and water levels attended to at intervals. Self-contained battery-electric locos have a longer endurance but will still need to stop for charging.

Station layouts can be very simple or very complex. They usually include some or all of the following features:

1 Crossover from 'up' to 'down' main line.
2 Passing loop so that a through train can overtake a stopping train.
3 Run-round loop so that the loco can be placed on the other end of the train for the return journey.
4 Bay platform for the use of a branch railcar or push-pull train whose engine does not need to run round.
5 Siding with platform and shed for unloading goods.
6 Siding(s) for unloading bulk loads such as coal.
7 Siding for parking of brake van while a train is remarshalled.
8 Headshunt to enable shunting of goods trains to take place without running on to the main line.
9 Turntable for turning tender engines (tank engines are not normally turned).
10 Facilities for coaling, watering, servicing and overnight stabling of locomotives.

Some possible layouts with these features numbered are illustrated in schematic form; they are drawn much shorter than in reality, like the diagram in a signal-box, to make the layout of the pointwork clearer. They are also shown straight, but nearly all stations in Britain are on a curve of some sort, and the model will be more realistic if built in this way. Even a straight station will look better if it is not parallel to the edge of the baseboard.

Full-size station layouts varied enormously, depending on the site available and the traffic they had to handle. Look at as many as you can and see how the facilities were fitted in — even now, when the goods sidings have been pulled up, you can usually see where they used to be. The 1/2500 series of Ordnance Survey maps actually show the track layouts at stations, often layouts that have been pulled up since they were drawn; these are very useful. Then ask yourself: why is the station there? What service was it meant to provide to the locality, what traffic did it handle, and what restrictions of cost and space influenced its design? Planning a layout in this way ensures that it will be convincing in appearance and fun to operate.

BASEBOARDS

No job on a model railway is more important than the baseboards. Rolling stock, track, scenery and electrics can be replaced if they prove unsatisfactory, but once the railway is on top of it there is very little that can be done about an unsatisfactory baseboard. It follows that this is one place in which you cannot afford to skimp.

The ideal sub-structure should be rigid and not move or distort with changes of temperature or humidity; it should not act as a sounding-board for the noise of trains, and if the layout is to be portable it must also be fairly light. These factors, and the ever-present one of cost, all act against each other, and have to be balanced according to the builder's needs and ability. Wood in some form is almost universally used for model railway baseboards; it is not unduly expensive, gives a good strength/weight and strength/cost ratio, and can be assembled fairly easily without specialised tools.

Plain timber has a grain and is much stronger along than across it; its movement with changes in humidity is also much greater across than along the grain. For this reason it is mostly confined

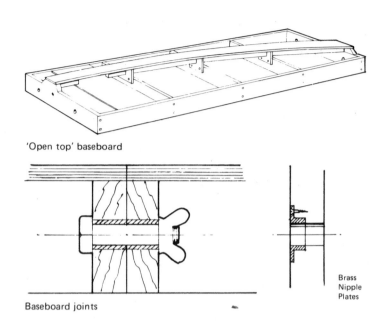

'Open top' baseboard

Baseboard joints

Brass
Nipple
Plates

to framing, where all the important dimensions lie along the grain. Most timber sold for building and do-it-yourself use is softwood and is seldom properly seasoned, and so will probably shrink appreciably, even along the grain, after assembly. Hardwoods are more expensive, depending on where you buy them, but more stable. A good compromise is to buy old timber (eg; floorboards) from demolition sites; such timber has had time to settle and, provided it is free from rot and woodworm, will give far less trouble than new wood. It is a good idea to 'condition' the wood in the layout room for a few weeks before assembling it, especially if the room has central heating.

Hardboard is not much good for track supports; it is too thin and flexible (though this can be an asset in modelling roads), needs a lot of bracing and 'drums' badly. Insulation boards of various types can be used but some will not hold nails or screws and they tend to sag. Chipboard is better but is heavy, and some grades disintegrate if they get damp. Blockboard is stiff but expensive and heavy; it can be useful in critical areas, for example, where there is a lot of pointwork, giving rigidity without a lot of bracing. Plywood is the best material; most durable of all is marine grade (BSS1088) but the waterproof exterior grade used by builders for shuttering is nearly as good and a lot cheaper, though not so pretty. All these materials can be shaped and assembled with the sort of basic woodworking tools that a home handyman will already have; there is no need for fancy carpentry, but joints should be glued and screwed, corner blocks being added where extra strength is desirable (at support points and the corners of sections).

Although we still call them baseboards, model railway sub-structures now seldom follow the old plan of a large flat table stiffened by framing. In the 'open top' system each section consists of a fairly deep frame with a number of cross-pieces carrying upstands which in turn support the track formations, cut from plywood. Roads are made in the same way but with lighter material and bases for buildings are fitted as necessary, the rest of the scenery then being filled in as described in Chapter 8. The advantages over the 'flat table' approach are the saving of material by concentrating it into those areas that really need it; better access; the ability to model scenery below as well as above track level; and the ease with which gradients can be built in. The plywood formations can best be cut out with a jig-saw attachment on an electric drill, and if extra stiffness seems necessary strips of ply or plain timber can be glued underneath between the upstands to make them into T-girders.

Even if the layout is not intended to be portable it is best to build it in sections in case you have to move house. The limit here is the size of section that can be got through the door or down the stairs. The sections of truly portable layouts are usually designed to fit a particular car (modules 4ft long will fit on the back seats of most saloons) and so tend to be smaller. Again a compromise: the fewer joints the better, but not if it makes the sections so big that they become unwieldy and get damaged each time they are moved.

The joints between sections should be made with well-fitting bolts and nuts through the end members of the frames. In joints that are to be undone often, the holes should be reinforced with

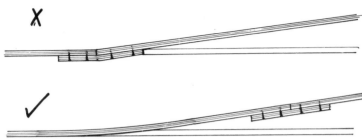

Installing gradients

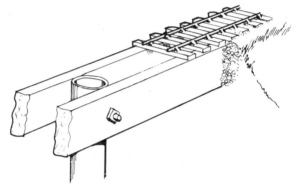

Substructure for line over garden

pieces of metal tube epoxy-glued in, or with the brass 'nipple plates' sold by electrical dealers. Ideally the formations should be laid right across the joint with the bolts in place and sawn along the joint line afterwards.

In a semi-permanent layout the supporting legs can be simply lengths of timber screwed to the framing, while the back edge can be plugged and screwed into the wall if other members of the family do not object. Layouts for exhibition use usually have folding legs (like those of a card table) to each section; it is a good idea to fit a levelling screw (a 3/8in or 1/2in Whitworth bolt) to the end of each leg, as the floors of exhibition halls are never level.

The height of the baseboard above the floor should be carefully considered. Models are most realistic if viewed at eye level, so track level should be about an inch below the operator's eye level when seated. This also usually results in a height convenient for access both underneath (for wiring and point rodding) and on top (for maintenance of track). On the other hand, the operation of a complicated layout is easier if you can see it all, which implies a lower baseboard — or a higher viewpoint. One answer is to have a high stool or chair for the operator and lower ones for spectators. Other factors such as the presence of a car or furniture may dictate a higher level.

Although an 'all level' railway is easier on the locos, gradients make it more interesting; most electric locos can pull reasonable loads up gradients up to about 1 in 50. To incorporate a gradient in an 'open top' system, you need only graduate the height of the upstands and bend the plywood formation to suit, adjusting with a little packing if necessary. Running is much smoother if the trains enter and leave gradients by a curve in the vertical plane rather than a sharp angle, so the transition from level to the full slope should be made in one piece, any necessary joints being either all on the level or all on a constant gradient.

The sub-structure for an outdoor railway can be built in the same way, with all woodwork well painted or creosoted, or the track can be laid directly on the ground like the prototype. Laying a line like this is quite practical and very interesting, but it is a long job — the formations must be well rammed, with plenty of broken stone for drainage, and left for six to twelve months to settle before final levelling and laying the track in a deep bed of ballast — and the resulting line will need quite a lot of maintenance to keep it level. One compromise method is to drive a series of posts into the ground, screw or bolt lengths of timber (say 4in x 1in) vertically either side and align these before fixing the track on top and then building up the ground to conceal the supports; or a concrete trough can be cast in sections and levelled up before filling with ballast and laying the track.

Although a garden line looks much better at ground level its operation involves a lot of bending or squatting. If the ground is on a slope the main station can be located at the lowest point, where the track will be on an embankment; some modellers dig a trench for the operator to stand in.

PERMANENT WAY

Although in recent years there has been a change to flat-bottom rail, standard British track up to the 1950s consisted of bullhead section steel rails attached to transverse wooden sleepers via cast chairs. In Gauges 0 and 1 this construction is usually reproduced, the chairs being white-metal castings threaded on to the rail and fixed to the sleepers with fine panel-pins. The sleepers are then pinned to longitudinal wooden battens or a plywood base.

In the smaller scales this kind of construction becomes rather fiddly and other methods have been devised. Most commercially-made track uses a moulded plastic base which incorporates the sleepers and rail fixings, into which the rail is threaded. The sleepers are joined together, so that a reasonable number can be made as a single moulding and depending on how this is done the track can be rigid or flexible. Nickel silver rail is generally used for its 'steely' colour, good electrical contact and easy soldering.

The simplest way to assemble a model railway is to fix sections of rigid track to the base. Most train-set manufacturers offer rigid track curved to various radii, usually 8 or 12 pieces to a circle, as well as straight track and points. Some also supply templates to help in planning the layout to scale. More complicated layouts usually require half and quarter sections of both curves and straights, and occasionally an odd fraction will be necessary; in this case the next longer available piece must be cut to length and the cut end provided with joiners. Do not try to make the joints line up by distorting the rest of the layout; this causes 'dog-legs' at the other joints and bad running.

Most modellers find commercial 'set' track formations too restricting and use flexible track, which is usually supplied in yard lengths and can be bent and cut to fit the layout. In 00 and N gauges there is a fair amount of standardisation, and most makes of rigid and flexible track can be joined together; but check before buying. Both rigid and flexible tracks are usually joined by tubular 'joiners' which push on to the feet of the rail-ends; these are made both in metal, and in plastic for joints which have to be insulated (see Chapter 10).

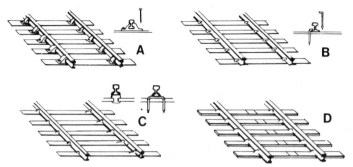

Methods of track laying: A, Bullhead rail in chairs; B, Flat bottom rail spiked down; C, Soldering to rivets or staples; D, Soldering to copper-clad sleepers

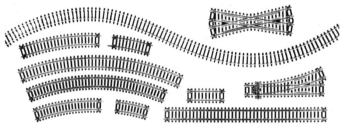

Flexible track and Setrack *(Peco)*

Many modellers lay their own track: because no ready-made track is available to their scale, to keep the cost down, to get a better appearance (eg; by using coarse-scale parts made for a smaller gauge) or simply for the fun of doing it. There are many methods: flat-bottom rail can be glued or spiked down, while bullhead rail can be fixed in chairs, soldered to pins, or soldered directly to copper-clad paxolin sleepers. This last method is very popular and gives a strong and easily-adjusted track fairly quickly.

A track gauge is necessary. Basically this is simply a block of metal cut to exactly the right thickness, though it can have clips or grooves to hold the rail upright and be cut away in the middle to clear other rails at pointwork; it can also be arranged to gauge check rail clearances and so on, like the roller gauges by Millholme Models shown in the photo.

In full-size track the ballast comes just about level with the sleeper tops, and when the model track is laid this has to be reproduced. If the track uses paper or veneer sleepers, a layer of ballast one grain thick will suffice, and this can be obtained easily by sprinkling ballast on a layer of glue or double-sided Sellotape. Methods which use thick sleepers need the ballast built up level with them; it is best to brush the ballast into position and then gently spray it with PVA glue (eg; Unibond) diluted in about ten times its volume of water. If the ballast bed is well soaked with this solution it will set very hard overnight. Aquarium sand is about the right size for ballast in N or TT gauges; coarser sand for 00, and fine 'chicken grit' (from a pet shop or farm supplier) for 0 and 1. Some modellers prefer a softer material such as powdered cork, which will do less damage if it gets into a loco mechanism. But any sort of ballast should be well fixed, at least in small scales, either by the dilute-glue method or by spraying with matt varnish after laying.

Some people like to lay their track on foam rubber to reduce noise. This works with coarse-scale track but fine-scale rail needs a firm support to keep it level; fix it to strips of thin plywood and place the foam rubber under that.

Using flexible or hand-laid track allows us to make a transition curve where straight track enters a curve. Ideally this should be a geometrical spiral, but a good approximation is 1½ coach-lengths at twice the radius of the main curve. Entering a curve this way not only looks better, but reduces 'buffer locking' with long vehicles.

For laying out fairly sharp curves a piece of string and a pencil will usually serve, but for very wide curves this method is unsatisfactory; the string, or even wire, may have too much stretch, or the centre may not be in the room at all. In this case, you can use 'track-setters' which are sold for the commoner track gauges and radii, buy 'railway curves' from a draughtsman's supply shop, or plot your own on pieces of stiff card or hardboard. If a lot of curved track is to be laid, it is well worth making a simple jig for positioning the sleepers.

Sharp curves that are normally taken at high speed are canted inwards ('super-elevated') in full size track; this is not necessary in

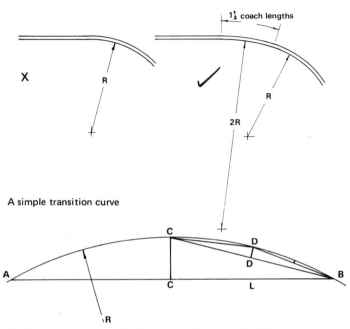

A simple transition curve

Plotting a curve whose radius is too large for trammels. Select a convenient length AB, less than about one-eighth the radius; call *half* its length L. The length of the perpendicular CC' at the mid-point of AB is given by $\dfrac{L^2}{2R}$

Now join AC' and BC' and erect perpendiculars at their mid-points; these will be equal to CC'/4. This operation can be repeated as many times as necessary; each time L is halved, the perpendicular is quartered. Finally draw a fair curve through all the points

a model because the mass of the trains is so much less, but it does improve the appearance. In an 'open top' structure it can easily be done by sloping the tops of the upstands supporting the trackbed. Sharp curves enable 'more railway' to be fitted into a given space but they are a nuisance in operation; trains both look better and run better on curves of large radius. In particular sharply curved S-bends should be avoided; even a few inches of straight track in between the two opposing curves makes a big difference.

Exact-scale 4mm trackwork on the North London Group layout. The scale rail section and fine flangeways contribute a great deal to the realism; but equally important is the 'flow' from straight to curve and the careful alignment which ensures trouble-free running *(P. Godfrey)*

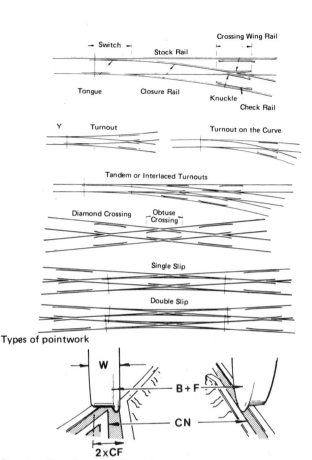

Types of pointwork

The vital dimensions of pointwork

*1 Wheel width W must always be more than twice the crossing flangeway
CF, so that some part of the wheel is always supported on either the wing
rail or the crossing nose and does not drop into the gap.*
*2 The check-rail gauge CN must always be equal to, or more than, the
wheel check gauge B + F, so that the check rail prevents the left-hand
flange from going the wrong side of the crossing.*
*3 Similarly, the dimension across the ends of the switch tongues must be
equal to, or less than, CN, so that the wheel passing through the open
switch does not hit the end of the tongue.*
Compare this diagram with the table in Chapter 2

Millholme roller track gauges

The simplest form of turnout is that in which a whole piece of track is slewed to line up with one set of rails or another. 'Stub-points' like this are sometimes used in narrow gauge systems, and the simplest toy trains traditionally use something similar, but the normal form of turnout is as shown in the diagram. In addition to plain turnouts, there are Y turnouts and turnouts on the curve, which are just the same except that both roads are curved; tandem or interlaced turnouts, diamond crossings, and single and double slips. Some of these look complicated, but if you study them carefully you will see that they are all made up of four items:

A **switch** consists of a pair of rails tapered to a knife edge so that they can divert wheels one way or the other.

A **common crossing** (Frog) allows one rail to cross another where the flangeways are on opposite sides.

An **obtuse or 'K' crossing** allows one rail to cross another where the flangeways are on the same side.

Check rails are always placed opposite a crossing to prevent the wheel flanges from going the wrong side of the crossing nose.

The diagram also shows the few simple rules which govern the dimensioning of any pointwork. These rules are already 'built into' the dimensions given in the table in Chapter 2; but understanding them helps to understand how any special pointwork operates and makes trouble-shooting easier. Again, if a lot of similar turnouts are to be made, it may be worth making a jig — though one reason for laying your own turnouts is that they *do not* all have to be the same.

A Gauge 0 wagon built from a Three Aitch, plastic kit and 'weathered' using a mixture of brush and spray techniques

A busy scene as two expresses pass in John Paige's 'Birchester' station. Virtually everything in the picture is built from commercially available kits (J. F. W. Paige)

Points can be operated by levers placed next to the switches, but it is more convenient to group the controls together as in a full-size signal-box. Where the turnout is only a few feet from the control position, it can be linked to the lever by piano wire in copper or brass tube (like a Bowden cable). For better appearance, the tubing can be run under the scenery. Where several electrical connections have to be changed over at the same time as the points are thrown, it is convenient to use a toggle or rotary switch as the control and make it operate the wire mechanically.

Where the distance from operating panel to turnout is too great or where they are on different baseboard sections, a point motor is used. This has two electro-magnets, one for each direction, and operates the points through a cam or pin-in-slot mechanism which prevents the spring of the switches from pushing the motor back when the control current is switched off. Because the electro-magnets need a lot of current to give sufficient force to operate the points, they can only be energised in short pulses; there are special 'passing contact' switches for this purpose, but a better way is to use contacts in the point motor to switch it off when it has thrown. Commercial ready-made turnouts sometimes have point motors built in, or are made so that they can be clipped on underneath.

LOCOMOTIVES

In the large scales there is some choice of motive power — electric, clockwork, steam or even diesel — and electrifying an outdoor layout brings its problems. The building of steam and diesel locos is too specialised to deal with here, and clockwork propulsion is also now a rather specialised subject since good clockwork mechanisms are very hard to obtain. Clockwork locos suffer from wear and tear due to the fairly energetic handling needed during winding; nevertheless several well-known Gauge 0 layouts are operated efficiently on spring-power alone. The

GWR 2-6-2 tank in 00 gauge *(Airfix Products)*

modern equivalent of the clockwork engine is the battery-electric; the loco carries a set of dry cells or rechargeable nickel-cadmium batteries and a controller and is recharged or the batteries changed during station stops. Dry battery propulsion is very expensive.

For indoor layouts in Gauge 0 and smaller, the electric loco is almost universal; and among these, all but a handful use 12-volt direct current, only Märklin remaining faithful to AC. The power can be fed to the loco by a third rail, either in the centre of the track or to one side, both running rails being used as a return; by 'stud contact', a series of studs or pins being fixed in the middle of the track and current being collected by a 'skate' made long enough always to make contact with at least one pin; or by insulating the running rails from each other and using one for each terminal of the supply. Three-rail and stud systems give more reliable contact, since all the loco wheels are available as a return contact and the shoe makes a rubbing (and thus self-cleaning) contact with the third rail; but the advantages of two-rail in appearance and simplicity have made it almost universal.

The typical ready-made loco has a body of either die-cast zinc alloy or moulded plastic, sometimes with extra detail parts added separately. The chassis is also usually a die-casting and the motor is made as a separate, detachable unit which drives one axle through a worm gear of a fairly high ratio. Lately some makers

Midland 2-4-0 built from a 4mm plastic kit *(Ratio)*

have returned to the earlier practice of making the motor an integral part of the chassis and using multi-stage spur gearing instead of a worm.

Both the appearance and performance of ready-made locos have improved enormously in recent years, but there is still quite a lot that the individual modeller can do to improve them, such as adding wire handrails where these are moulded into the body, toning down a too-shiny or historically incorrect paint scheme or fitting etched brass nameplates instead of transfers where appropriate. Below the footplate, the driving wheels may have to be re-profiled or replaced to suit a finer track standard, the motionwork — often very sketchily represented — can be improved, and dummy sideframes incorporating spring detail, ashpan and so on cut from thin metal (or even card) and fixed to the sides of the chassis. It is surprising what a difference this last addition can do for a loco's appearance, especially on an 'eye-level' layout.

Most commercial locos are undergeared. Small motors run best at high speeds (15 - 30,000rpm) whereas the wheels of steam locos seldom exceeded 400rpm. The step-down ratio can often be increased by fitting a replacement gear set (most Triang-Hornby locos only need a single-start worm in place of the original two-start one). Worm gears of high ratio waste a lot of power in friction, and the teeth are smaller and more critical in adjustment of meshing, so for a very high ratio, such as would be needed for

The 7.35 sets out for Waterloo on a layout operated on a train-based timetable. The clock to the left of the control panel has two speeds; normal time for shunting and double-speed for long timetable runs

Steam among the rhododendrons — the special appeal of a live-steam garden railway (D. Simpson)

LNER 'N7' 0-6-2 tank (above) partly assembled and (below) completed and painted. White metal cast kit by Wills Finecast

'Evening Star' Class 9F by Hornby has jointed coupling rods to assist in getting round sharp curves; because of the large amount of 'daylight' between boiler and mainframes in the prototype, it is powered by a ring-field motor in the tender *(MacLeish Associates)*

a shunting or goods engine with a low top speed, it is better to retain the original worm gear and drive it through a spur reduction gear of 2 or 3 to 1. This can sometimes be fitted in quite simply by gently reaming out the worm bore until it runs freely on the motor shaft and driving it by a double gear train like that which moves the hour hand of a clock.

Electrical pick-up can also often do with improvement. Ideally every wheel of a loco, including bogie, pony-truck and tender wheels should have a metal rim and some form of collector. Like a milking stool, a rigid loco chassis only makes firm contact with the track at three points, and if the one wheel which is making contact on one side hits a spot of dirty track, the loco will stall. This is why pick-up via the wheels of a sprung bogie is especially helpful.

Some people also like to fit flywheels to the motors of their locos. Running at high speed, these greatly increase the apparent momentum of the engine and enable it to coast smoothly through patches of rough or dirty track. These refinements take time and care to fit but make a big difference to the smooth, reliable running of an engine.

Parts for most of these improvements can be bought at a model railway shop, and you can also buy a very wide range of kits. The simplest of these are the same as the ready-made locos and need only a few minutes' work with a screwdriver to assemble; but most consist of castings of low-melting point lead alloy which are assembled with epoxy glue (Araldite), cyanoacrylate glue (Loctite, Zap, X-30) or, if you are careful, solder. Some kits also include parts made from sheet brass by photo-etching; some are entirely made this way and can, of course, be soldered without difficulty. Most of these kits are very accurate and, with care, will make up into really fine models; read the instructions (both for the kit *and the adhesive)* carefully and do not rush the job.

Kits are often designed to fit on a commercial chassis but sometimes one has to be specially built. The frame plates can be cut out of sheet brass with a piercing saw, two pieces being clamped or soldered together and drilled and shaped as one. Brass bushes are soldered into the axle holes, the frames are screwed to

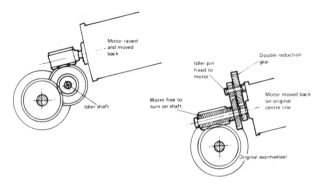

Fitting extra gearing into a locomotive. A, Idler shaft; B, 'Hour hand' gearing to worms

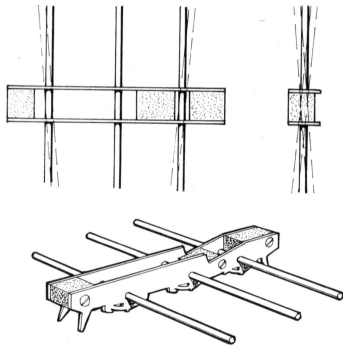

Lining-up a locomotive chassis

Basically simple scenery carefully blended into the backscene gives a natural effect despite the narrowness of the baseboard

A ballast train rumbles out of Heckmondwike on the North London Group layout. Note the carefully-observed details: weeds in the headshunt, the ground signal, the corrugated iron hut and the small differences between basically standard wagons *(P. Godfrey)*

Even small and unspectacular engines can make fine models. This 4mm model of the GWR's well-loved '48xx' class was built nearly 20 years ago by Guy Williams for the Pendon Museum *(P. Williams)*

metal or plastic spacers, and wheels and motor are attached as in the commercial job. Make the coupling rods *first* and use them as a drilling jig for the axle holes to ensure that these match exactly; that is really the only tricky part. Get two or three lengths of 'silver steel' rod the same diameter as the axles and thread them through the axle holes to make sure these are properly lined up before drilling the fixing holes in the spacers.

Sooner or later you will want a model of an engine for which there is no kit. It may be possible to modify the kit for a different engine by the same designer by making some parts yourself, or the whole thing may have to be built from scratch. It is not as difficult as it looks, and there is great satisfaction in watching the model grow out of raw materials. If you have not the tools or the skill to work in metal, try card or polystyrene sheet; some very fine locos have been built from both these materials. Most of the 'bits and bobs' like chimneys, buffers, handrail knobs and steam fittings, can be bought as castings from the model shop. Get as much information as you can; never trust a single drawing, but check the details with as many photos as you can find of the chosen prototype. Many classes of engine had a lot of variation or were rebuilt several times, so if possible, choose a single example of the class at a given date and model that.

ROLLING STOCK

What kind of rolling stock you have on your railway depends very much on what the line is supposed to do; some lines carried passengers almost exclusively while others concentrated on goods traffic. For an interesting railway there should be a sensible mixture of both, with perhaps some justification for special vehicles; if your model is set in a coalfield, you will need some old coaches reserved for miners' trains, or if there is a big engineering works nearby there will be a need for special wagons to carry large, heavy loads.

Nowadays both coaches and wagons are rather standardised but before nationalisation — and even more before the 1923 grouping — each company had an individual style of building wagons and coaches which added a lot of interest to the railway scene, especially when 'foreigners' worked through. This is probably why so many modellers — even those too young to remember the prototype — like to model the pre-war railway scene. Whatever your choice, let there be a reason for each vehicle being there, just as with everything else on the railway.

As with locos, there is a splendid variety of rolling stock available either ready-made or in kit form. Some of the commercial stock needs only fine-scale wheels and a little repainting to look 'at home' on a scale layout. Before the War there were enormous numbers of 'private owner' coal wagons in use, with many interestingly individual liveries; it is fun to introduce some of these, using names of firms appropriate to the location and even slipping in the occasional invention of one's own! Most of these wagons were to a Railway Clearing House standard design, usually with either a 5-plank or 7-plank body, and there are several excellent models of both types available which only need repainting. In some areas there is a lot of cattle traffic, while in others at certain times one sees long trains of vans carrying perishable traffic — fruit, vegetables or fish. In 00 gauge some really beautiful kits are available for all these vehicles, in both metal and plastic; there are even some etched-brass kits for the large GWR bogie vans ('Siphons' and 'Monsters') that cost nearly as much as a small loco but make magnificent models

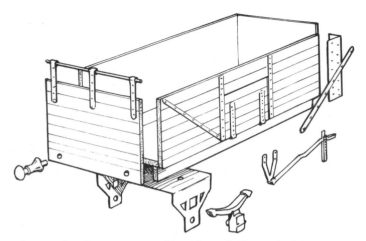

Construction of an open wagon. The sides, ends, floor and solebars are cut from thin plywood; the strapping and corner plates can be bought or made from card or metal foil, and the axleguards and other fittings bought, usually as white-metal castings

when complete. Except for special-purpose vehicles, there seems to be very little point in scratch-building goods stock in 00 unless you like doing so; but it is interesting to bring in a little variety by making small changes to show the detail differences between early and late batches of the same basic design, or the modifications that were made to certain vehicles. Some kits include optional parts to help with this.

Passenger rolling stock is not so well catered for commercially. Most firms merely make a basic coach body and offer it in several different company colours. To build up a really convincing stock of coaches, even in 00 gauge, you will have to do some work, either assembling kits or modifying commercial coaches. Grafar suburban coaches and the older Triang 'main line' stock can be modified into all sorts of convincing models, using as much of the basic structure as is suitable and adding new parts or details — even completely new sides — cut from polystyrene sheet. Cast bogie kits and other accessories are again available from model shops.

An LMS full brake van (4mm scale) built from a Mallard Models etched brass kit. While not ideal for the novice, kits like this make up into models of really excellent appearance

Langs Puddle station and village forms one end of the 2mm scale layout built by the late J. J. Langridge along the top of a built-in bookcase

(Above) GWR 'Toad' brake van (Below) 10ft wheelbase wagon underframe. Plastic kits by Ratio

(Above) LMS (ex Midland) coach from a plastic kit (Ratio) and (below) SR brake-third built from a 'King's Cross' wooden kit by Guy Williams *(P. Williams)*

For vehicles that really have to be built from scratch, there is a wide choice of materials. Wood is still very popular for goods vehicle bodies, especially the thin birch ply sold by model aircraft shops. Card — not cheap strawboard, but the fine-grained card sold by artists' suppliers — was equally popular, but has largely been eclipsed by polystyrene sheet (Plastikard) which is light, strong, damp-proof, easily worked and easily assembled with a solvent cement such as 'Mek-Pak'. For parts which need to be strong but thin — brake gear, for example — metal is still the best material; brass, nickel-silver, tinplate and even steel all have their uses. Epoxy and cyanoacrylate glues will stick metal to any of the other materials listed, but it may be better to use screws so that the different parts can be separated for cleaning and painting.

The weight of rolling stock is surprisingly uncritical. White-metal kit vehicles are generally rather heavy, while plastic ones are usually very light and the kits often include a ballast plate. What is more important is that they should run freely and that all the vehicles in a given train should weigh about the same, so that the heaviest ones do not pull the light ones off the track on curves.

A wagon or coach that does not run is no use to a full-size railway and not much to a model one. Nowadays more attention is paid to running; most proprietary models and kits have pin-point axles which run with very little friction, either in the material of which the underframe is made or in special brass or bronze bearing cups. In larger scales pin-points are not so popular and free running is obtained by reducing the diameter of the axle end, polishing it carefully and lining the axlebox with PTFE tubing. (PTFE is a plastic with a very 'slippery' surface). If a wagon or coach will not roll on a gradient of about 1 in 100 it needs attention.

Just as important is track-holding. Even on fine-scale track, provided it is reasonably well laid, springing or equalisation (making the underframe flexible so that all four wheels sit firmly on the rail) is not really necessary for trouble-free running, but accurate building is important. Check each wagon or coach bogie to see that the axles are parallel and at right-angles to the centre-line; place it on a surface plate or a piece of glass to check

'Siphon H' van built from a Mallard Models etched brass kit. *(P. Williams)*

A fine example of a scratch-built special-purpose wagon: a GWR 'Cordon' gas tank wagon built by Tony Smith in 4mm scale *(P. Williams)*

for 'wobble', and roll it along a smooth, flat surface (such as a Formica table-top) to see that it runs straight without 'crabbing'. Most commercial vehicles are good in this respect, but when you assemble a kit it is most important to get this part right even if it takes some time.

Springing does, however, improve the appearance of a moving train; small-scale coaches, being so light, tend to jerk visibly over all but the most perfect track if unsprung, and when you have gained a bit of experience in kit-building and scratch-building you may like to try a sprung vehicle, to see whether the improvement is worth the extra effort. There are many different ways of

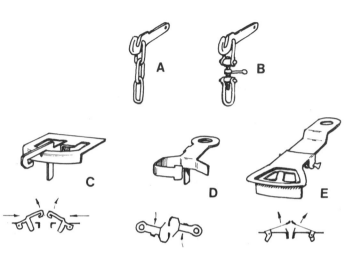

Types of coupling: A, scale three-link (for wagons); B, scale screw type (for locos and coaches); C, Triang/Hornby; D, Peco Simplex; E, Rivarossi

springing a vehicle, most of them nothing like the prototype; as with choosing a scale, the best thing is to try several and decide which is best for you on the basis of the results.

There are a lot of different sorts of coupling, varying from the prototype 3-link or screw type which looks good but is very fiddly to use, to the rather unsightly automatic types fitted to commercial models. In most cases the latter are much bigger than they need to be for a 'scale' layout with reasonable curves, and there are some smaller ones which still work well while not being so ugly. The Rivarossi type is particularly good but not very easy to obtain, while Peco produce a 'buck-eye' type which has stood the test of time. Many modellers prefer automatic couplings because the layout can be operated 'untouched by human hand' using mechanical ramps or electro-magnets to uncouple as required. A busy terminal or junction layout will need a reliable auto-coupler, while the 'wayside watcher' type of model can work quite happily with scale 3-link couplings, all the fiddling being done 'behind the scenes'. Again, it is a matter of choosing what suits you and your particular layout best.

SCENERY AND BUILDINGS

It is usual to leave the scenic work on a model railway until after the track has been laid and 'de-bugged', although some builders feel that, as the prototype scenery was there long before the railway, a more realistic effect can be created by modelling them in the same order. Certainly one needs to think about what the country looked like before the railway was built, what natural features caused the railway to be aligned as it was and what the prototype engineers did about them. Either way, it is essential to design the scenery as an integral part of the layout and not just stick it on as an afterthought.

The best thing to do, if you can manage it, is to spend a holiday in the area in which your layout is to be set and 'get the feel' of the local landscape: whether the hills are rugged or rounded, the seashore steep cliffs or flat marsh, and so on. Photograph or sketch interesting corners of towns and villages — not necessarily to be copied exactly, but to give you a starting-point. Look for the little differences that give the place its identity: the local industries, the odd-shaped lamp-post, the pub with the unusual name or the colour of the local stone.

If you look at almost any piece of prototype trackwork you will find it is not at ground level. Even in country that appears to be flat, the line is nearly always on a low embankment or in a shallow cutting; roads often take advantage of these small undulations to cross over or under the railway. This is the great advantage of 'open top' construction; with no flat baseboard top there is no temptation to model totally flat countryside, and the result is more natural.

The chief use of tunnels — or at least tunnel mouths — on a model railway is to create a scenic barrier, usually at the point where the 'scenic' part of the model ends and the line passes into a 'fiddle yard'. But tunnels on a full-size line are not undertaken lightly; it is not at all convincing to have the line tunnel neatly through an isolated pimple-like hill when by a simple diversion it could have gone round it on the level. To be realistic, a hill with a tunnel must be high enough — or at least imply that it gets high enough — for a tunnel to be obviously more economical than a deep cutting. If your model is set in flat country a road bridge with well-embanked road approaches makes a more convincing barrier than a tunnel.

Apart from the ever present requirement of low cost, scenic materials need to be durable and easily applied, and not to create dust. Various types of plaster (Artex in particular) are popular; the usual scheme is to build up a rough framework of wire mesh, crumpled paper or strips of card and to lay over this gauze, tarlatan or paper tissues well soaked in fairly wet plaster to build up a shell 1/8in or more thick. The plaster can be 'sculptured' with a palette knife or brush into shapes suggesting various types of rock; these can be moulded separately, or pieces of cork, bark or coal used, depending on the effect required. The plaster should be brushed well over all the surrounding woodwork so that in the completed model no bare wood shows; even when painted, its grain will usually show and spoil the effect.

Another useful material is resin and glassfibre as sold for repairing car bodywork. Again a temporary support of wire mesh is built up; the glass mat is then cut into pieces about 6in square, which are impregnated with resin and hardener and applied in the same way as the plastered gauze. It is tougher and more suitable for portable layouts and bonds to structural woodwork much better than plaster. Wear old clothes and protective gloves when working with glassfibre.

Man-made slopes, such as embankments and cuttings, are usually too regular to be reproduced with a wire form and the best solution is to cut them from cardboard and then cover them with plaster-and-gauze or GRP as appropriate.

Bare earth (ploughland) can be represented with painted plaster but most of the landscape will need to be covered in 'grass'. In very small scales this too can be painted plaster, but in 00 and larger some texture is needed. For small areas chamois leather, roughened with a wire brush, looks fine, but it is expensive; most modellers use surgical lint bought in large rolls and dyed in bulk. Do not just use green dye; there is a lot of brown and yellow in grass too, and the colour varies a lot with the type of grass (pasture, moorland, waste ground). Coloured flock powders are sold for use as grass but are very expensive for

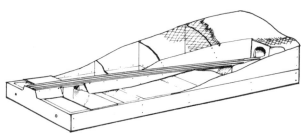

Scenic completion of the layout section shown in Chapter 4

Above: hardboard or ply formers installed, cardboard slopes of cutting and embankment pinned on, wire netting laid on and tarlatan/plaster or glassfibre/resin covering started. Note the cardboard lining to the tunnel. River bed painted and varnished.

Below: terrain structure complete and covered with 'grass' material; river banks faired in and bridge installed. Masonry tunnel mouth, boundary fences, trees and bushes fixed in position. Scenic backgrounds painted on hardboard and attached to back and end

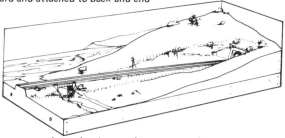

large areas — and nearly always the wrong colour.

There are many ways of making trees: the skeleton can be a natural twig or heather stem, or a bunch of wires twisted together for the main trunk and splayed out a few at a time for branches. The smaller branches and twigs can be steel wool or dyed lichen, with a final dressing of dyed sawdust 'leaves' after painting the skeleton with dark brown or grey gloss paint. Dark green or brown sponge chopped up, 'Scotchbrite' pot scourers, tea leaves, natural moss and dried flower heads are all possible materials.

Smooth water is not hard to model. A really clear trout-stream can be modelled with 'clear pouring plastic' (from a handicraft shop) but for the murkier waters of most rivers or canals it is better to apply several coats of gloss varnish over brownish-green

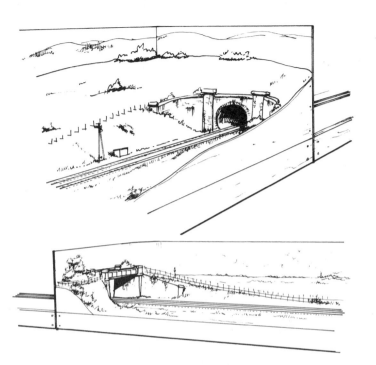

Tunnel (top) a road bridge, (bottom) as scenic barriers

gloss paint on a grain-free base such as hardboard. Waves are very difficult to model convincingly in a 'frozen' state and are best avoided.

Nearly all natural surfaces have a matt finish, so poster or acrylic paints are best for scenic work. Do not use the paint too thick or it will cover up the texture; if you can spray it, so much the better (see Chapter 9). Most layouts need a backscene to make them look finished; several firms supply these printed in colour for various scales, or you can paint your own on hardboard.

The style of buildings must suit the supposed locale and period of the layout; as with the scenery, it is best to visit the area and make sketches and photographs of typical buildings. Most towns

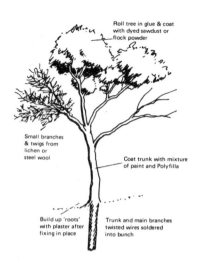

Roll tree in glue & coat with dyed sawdust or flock powder

Small branches & twigs from lichen or steel wool

Coat trunk with mixture of paint and Polyfilla

Build up 'roots' with plaster after fixing in place

Trunk and main branches twisted wires soldered into bunch

Making trees

just grew rather than being planned, so there will be buildings which have obviously been squeezed into odd-shaped sites; including a few of these will make your town much more credible than a straight row of rectangular boxes. There are a lot of very good building kits made in printed card and plastic; the latter are too glossy as supplied, but can be toned down with matt paints. Do not make all the buildings up exactly to the kit instructions; it is more fun to mix kit parts (some of which can be bought separately) with others scratch-built from card or polystyrene sheet, and produces a more realistic result.

Model buildings need to be fairly well braced with internal walls to keep them from bulging (except, of course, in models of old houses where the walls are *meant* to bulge — these will probably remain obstinately straight). If you plan to install lighting, at least the inner layer of the walls should be of black card or styrene so that the light does not shine through.

Buildings which are just placed on their bases usually show an unsightly gap at the bottom. It is much better to extend the walls a little below street level and provide each building with a well-fitting card 'socket' into which it is plugged.

A street scene assembled from Superquick card kits *(J. F. W. Paige)*

This gantry-mounted signal cabin was scratch-built from Plastikard by Len Folkard. It is to 2mm/ft scale and only about the size of a matchbox, but has a slated roof, handrails and guttering detail

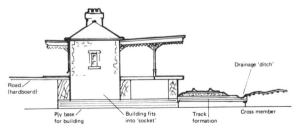

Fitting a model building into the 'landscape'

Even in 00 scale a textured surface, such as embossed brick, looks better than plain printed brickpaper, and if you have the patience to do it, a roof tiled or slated with strips of thin paper looks far better than flat 'tile paper'. It is amazing how much ordinary brickpaper is improved by just picking out the odd brick here and there in slightly different colours. Green moss round a cracked gutter pipe; yellow lichen on a slate roof; soot at the top of a tunnel mouth; all these little touches can give life to a model, but do not overdo them. Again, apart from the woodwork, all surfaces need a matt paint.

The best material for buildings for outdoor layouts is polystyrene sheet, which stands up to the weather remarkably well. Plastic building kits also stand up well and their bright glossy colours tone down after a season or two. The imaginative gardener with a Gauge 1 line can really have 'working scenery' with carefully-trimmed grass, low-lying plants and miniature trees.

Any railway needs people, and most need road vehicles. These can be bought in various scales; some Continental figures are beautifully detailed if rather expensive. You can sometimes save money by buying them unpainted. Once again, you can add a lot of individuality to your models by simple changes such as interchanging the top and bottom halves of two figures or putting them in different situations — a policeman's raised arm, for example, could equally well be painting a wall or sign or cleaning a window. The horses and figures made for war-gaming can also be adapted for model railway use.

PAINTING, WEATHERING AND LIGHTING

Assembling and painting a model railway is like painting a picture, but in three dimensions and without the artist's problems of establishing perspective and relief on a flat canvas. The most satisfying models are those in which the whole scene has been carefully blended in to give a sense of unity. To do this requires

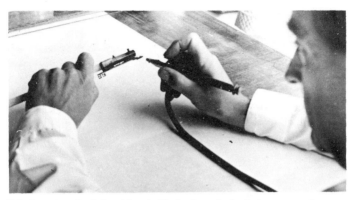

Painting a loco body by airbrush. Notice how the body is supported on a wooden handle to avoid touching the primed surfaces

A wagon set up for lettering. White undercoat and artists' oils are mixed in a disposable plastic palette for the desired 'off white' shade; the vehicle is securely chocked with a full-size template immediately above and a photo ready for reference. The blocks of wood give a firm rest for the painter's hand at the same level as the wagon side

the artist's ability to observe, to analyse exactly why things look as they do and to work out how this appearance can be translated into terms of coloured pigment. Some people are born with this knack but most can learn it if they are prepared to try. Many of the most useful materials come from artists' supply shops.

LNER brake composite coach, scratch-built in Plastikard by E. R. H. Francis. The varnished teak livery of LNER coaches was beautiful but is a real challenge to the model-painter *(P. Williams)*

Most items of railway equipment — locos, rolling stock and the wooden and steel parts of buildings — were painted with gloss paint to give ease of cleaning and protection against weather. Coaches and locos were regularly cleaned and repainted and so kept their gloss, at least to some extent, but wagons soon faded to a near-matt finish. Building materials — stone, brick, concrete — and nearly all natural vegetation have matt surfaces. Even when painting locos and coaches, it is better to start with matt paint and varnish them when finished; lining and lettering are easier to apply on a matt base than on a glossy one.

There is not much to choose between the best brushed and sprayed paintwork, but an airbrush — a small spraygun giving very fine control — is a great time-saver and gives a thinner, more even coat. A good airbrush will have separate controls for air and paint supplies, and with practice you can make it draw a thin line or cover a wide area; the air supply can be provided by a car tyre pump, a canister of compressed 'aerosol' gas or a small compressor. The last item can sometimes be salvaged from a scrapped refrigerator.

Brushed paintwork is only as good as the brush that applies it. In an artist's quality red sable brush (recognisable by the light red-brown colour of the hairs) each bristle tapers to a point so that the brush itself can be quite large (and so hold a good supply of paint) and still be able to paint a fine line; they are made down to about size 000 but a carefully selected No 1 or 2 is quite small enough for lining and lettering even in 2mm scale. Sable hair has a 'spring' which gives good control. Eventually the fine 'point' hairs wear down and the brush becomes stubby; it can then be demoted to scenic and weathering use and for painting underframes, which would quickly ruin a new brush because of all the sharp corners and crevices. A good brush is worth looking after; wash all the colour out after use with two or three changes of the appropriate thinner and *then wash out the thinner* with soap and water until the lather is pure white; rinse it, stroke the bristles into a point, and leave it to dry standing point-upwards in a jar.

Surface preparation is very important. Where you want the grain of wood to show (eg; in a wagon) the paint can be applied direct, but a wooden coach body will need one or more coats of 'sanding sealer' with rubbing down between coats (best done before adding the fine details). Plastic models pick up a greasy coating during moulding and assembly and need to be well washed in a detergent solution (not too hot) and thoroughly rinsed and dried before painting. The same treatment, in hotter water and with vigorous scrubbing with an old toothbrush and an abrasive cleaner (Vim, Ajax) serves to remove grease and flux from metal models and to 'key' the surface for painting. Fingermarks at this stage will waste all the good work, so it is best to attach the model to a 'handle' so that it can be worked on without touching its surface.

Metal models should be given a 'priming' coat to stick the main colour to the metal. Grey cellulose primer as used on cars, thinned and sprayed as a light 'mist' coat so that it does not clog up the detail, is satisfactory; there are also etching primers which 'bite' into the metal (do not spray these) or you can treat the whole model with 'gun blue' or 'Hobby Black' which gives brass, nickel-silver and steel a tough black oxide deposit which holds paint well. Another good idea is to use matt black cellulose first on all the black parts, following with Humbrol for the coloured areas; any colour that strays over the line can then be wiped off with white spirit without spoiling the black.

The slow drying of artists' oil paints can be useful in lining or lettering; 'Liquin' is a useful medium for mixing them to a lining consistency. Alternatively there are retarding media available for

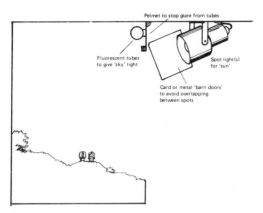

Pelmet to stop glare from tubes

Fluorescent tubes
to give 'sky' light

Spot light(s)
for 'sun'

Card or metal 'barn doors'
to avoid overlapping
between spots

Lighting a layout

use with acrylics. There are some very good transfers of both 'water-slide' and 'dry' types for the lettering and crests of the major companies but for wagon lettering hand-painting is best. Do not use pure white for wagon lettering — light grey looks more natural. Leave the lettered vehicle to dry for several days before varnishing; then apply a thin coat of artists' picture varnish and matt varnish, mixed to give the desired amount of gloss. Most matt varnishes need to be warmed before applying.

Most of the materials used for scenery are fairly porous and so will take poster or water colour well. Artists' oils can be used, but the new acrylic paints are quicker-drying and take well on plastics. For locos and rolling stock Humbrol and Precision Paints make ranges of ready-mixed 'Company' colours which can be brushed or sprayed, but for scenery you will need a basic 'palette' of colours, which can be mixed to give any shade you need: Lamp Black or Ivory Black, Cadmium Yellow, White, Cadmium Red, Burnt Sienna, Sap Green, Burnt Umber, Ultramarine and Yellow Ochre.

Ready-made models are invariably supplied in 'ex works' condition, shiny and new. After a few days in service a full-size 'vehicle' picks up a coating of dust from the ballast, which is thickest on the underframe and is usually a light grey-brown colour; while the roof collects a coating of soot. The sides of coaches are washed quite often and so stay fairly clean and shiny long after the underframe has become a matt khaki shade and the roof matt black. Wagons are not washed (except by rain) so the dust settles all over, especially in the corners, and projecting edges of metalwork get tinged with rust as the paint gets chipped off.

The representation of these effects, known as 'weathering', is one of the most important ingredients of a realistic model railway. There are two principal ways of applying it; a light 'mist' of the dust colour can be sprayed at long range obliquely to the surface with the airbrush, or fairly dry paint can be applied with a light flicking action using an old, stumpy brush. Keep a tissue handy to wipe off the excess if you overdo it.

With one exception, all weathering effects are matt; the exception is spillage of oil round axleboxes, tank wagon fillers and diesel sheds, reproduced with a mixture of black paint and gloss varnish.

Track needs painting too; apart from the rusty side of the rails the ballast colour varies with the material used, how long it has been there and the type of traction (steam, electric or diesel) using the line.

The colour of objects seen at a fair distance is lighter and bluer than those close by. This does not occur over the small distances involved in a model, and some (though not the author) think that 'scale colour' should include some degree of lightening to reproduce this effect. While one could get an impression of distance by toning down the colours of the remoter parts of the scenery in this way — and certainly those of the backscene — it is hardly practical on rolling stock and locos.

Lighting in the layout room is most important. Some paints — notably ultramarine — change colour under fluorescent lighting, and painting should always be done by daylight if possible or by a strong tungsten light as second best. Similarly, although a moderate amount of fluorescent lighting is useful as a 'sky' light, the main, or 'key' light of a layout should be a filament lamp or lamps — ideally a series of spotlights arranged and masked so that they do not overlap and no object throws two shadows. Since the sun is always south of us the direction of the key-light will subconsciously tell the viewer 'which way round' the layout is.

ELECTRIFICATION AND CONTROL

Most model railways in 00 and smaller gauges use two-rail electrical supply; that is, the two rails are insulated from each other and form the 'feed' and 'return' conductors. The alternative method, using either a third rail or a line of contact studs for the feed, is still commonly used in Gauges 0 and 1. Two-rail, of course, looks better, and none of the locomotive's power is wasted in dragging along the rubbing contact of a shoe or skate; but there are a few problems involved, mainly in the change of polarity needed when a train changes direction via a 'return loop'.

In a three-rail system all the running rails are bonded together and all one has to do is to provide conductor rails or studs joined all round the layout. With two-rail pointwork, at each common crossing the 'feed' rail of one track has to cross the 'return' of the other. The simple answer to this is to make the whole of the crossing of insulating material or cut insulating gaps either side of it, but this means pieces of 'dead' rail which can cause locos to stall as they pass over the points.

A more certain solution is to make the crossing 'live' and connect it via a change-over switch to one rail or the other, thus ensuring an unbroken feed right through the turnout. The switch is often dispensed with and the contact of the switch tongues with their stock rails used instead, but pieces of dust and ballast can easily put this kind of switching out of action; there is also a risk of metal wheels shorting against the open tongue as they pass, unless the throw of the tongues is made quite a bit overscale. The best way is to use a proper switch with self-cleaning and possibly enclosed contacts, either ganged to the point throwbar or itself used as a lever.

If the track at the 'toe' of the point is connected to the power supply, the two diverging tracks are automatically switched by this method; both rails of the track for which the points are not set are connected to the same side of the supply, so a loco on that track will not move until the turnout is set for it. If a whole fan of turnouts are wired in this way, the switching is automatic; only that siding for which the route is set receives current.

If the power feed is connected to the track at the 'heel' end of the turnout, this method does not work. In most layouts there will be one obvious place where the feed is best connected; any turnouts which are left 'the wrong way round' can then be provided with fresh feeds at their toes — possibly via section switches — and insulating gaps made in the rails to avoid shorting the controllers when the road is wrongly set. The gaps should be placed where it is unlikely that rolling-stock will be parked, so that metal wheel rims do not short out the gaps.

A large layout will probably have several operators, each responsible for a certain area and each having his own controller. The track is divided into sections, each fed through a switch so that it can be connected to any appropriate controller. This is known as 'Cab Control'; the 'signalman' sets up the routes and allocates a 'cab' to drive that train for the whole of its journey.

By using a three-pole change-over switch, turnouts can be wired so that the **toe** takes its power from either of the tracks at the heel end. Using this and the simple 'toe feed' circuits, any track formation can be wired so that the supply is connected to the whole of the selected route and no section switches (other than dead-ends) are necessary. As an example, consider the station shown, where three controllers are provided, one for Yard and one each for Up and Down main lines. A Down goods train can cross on to the Up line and thence into a selected siding in the yard, all on the Down controller; when the crossovers are returned to 'Normal', the Yard controller takes it over, leaving the main-line controllers free to deal with through trains, and eventually it can leave on the Up line under the control of the Up Main controller.

A similar system — Linked-Section Control — makes use of the signals to switch controllers. Basically, when a home signal is at 'danger' the track leading up to it is connected to a local controller, but when it is at 'clear' the track is linked through to the section ahead. In this way a length of line is automatically connected to the last controller in the sequence, and trains can be driven all the way up to the next 'stop' signal, the signals behind being set to 'danger' and freeing the local controllers for the next move.

It is a bit more complicated to wire a layout like this, but once

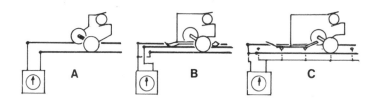

Methods of electrification, A Two-rail, B Three-rail, C Stud-contact

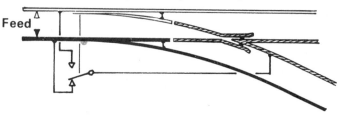

Feed

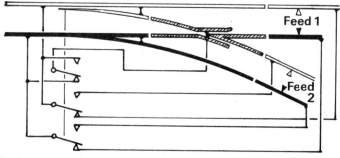

Feed 1

Feed 2

Toe feed and heel feed methods of wiring two-rail points

it is done you do not have to think about the electrics at all; you just set the routes and drive the trains. The (supposedly) difficult part only has to be done once, and afterwards both you and your fellow-operators will find the layout easier and more fun to operate.

The 12-volt DC supply required by most model locos is obtained from the mains via a transformer and rectifier. The

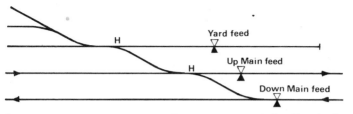

Controllers selected by point setting. The two turnouts labelled H are heel-fed as in 'b' of the previous figure

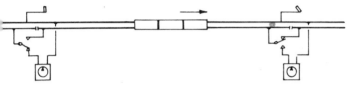

Linked section control

simplest form of speed control is simply a variable resistance in series with the supply; this works well enough at high speeds but, due to the characteristics of small motors, is not very reliable at low speeds. The variable transformer ('Powermaster') is better, because its output voltage is less affected by the amount of current being taken at any given setting. Even better are some types of transistor controller which, besides giving an output almost independent of current demand, incorporate overload protection circuits and in some cases facilities for gradual starting and stopping. Best of all are the latest types of transistor controller with 'feedback' which senses the small voltage generated by the rotating motor and corrects the output to maintain exactly the required speed.

Most small motors stick more or less when starting, partly due to friction and partly to their being designed down to a price. Pulse power, whereby almost the full power-pack output is applied in a series of short pulses, gives the motor a series of sharp 'kicks' to get it moving without the mean current being sufficient for it to run fast once started. Pulse power is useful but usually causes motors to get hotter than they do on DC for the same speed.

Point motors and signal solenoids use low-voltage AC or DC, and commercial controllers often provide suitable auxiliary outlets for this purpose. However, if there are a lot of these items, it may be better to provide a separate power pack.

There are a number of electronic systems on the market which enable several locos to run independently without track sectioning. The track is fed with a constant supply and each loco is fitted with an electronic module which in effect combines a controller with a tiny receiver 'tuned' to the signals sent along the track (not broadcast) by its own controller. Such systems appear likely to cost more than the section-switches they replace, but could be useful where the layout includes a large loco depot which would otherwise need a great many isolated sections, or an incline involving the use of banking engines.

Ready-made locos usually include suppressors to cut down TV interference. In most cases a miniature ceramic condenser of about .005 microfarad, connected as close to the motor brushes as possible, will reduce interference to an acceptable level, but in severe cases a small choke in each motor lead may also be necessary. These can be bought from a radio parts dealer. In exceptionally bad cases it may be necessary to connect small condensers across the track at intervals.

The electrical side of model railways is quite an interesting subject in its own right, and it is well worth while learning at least the basics of electrical theory (via a suitable text-book from the local library).

OPERATION

For the solo owner-operator virtually 'anything goes' but realistic and railwaylike operation is more satisfying. As soon as more than one person is involved, some sort of 'rule book' becomes almost essential so that each knows what to expect from the other. At almost any exhibition you can see the contrast between the muddle and intermittent operation of those who are just

An end-to-end TT gauge layout some 30ft long, built by the Malmesbury 3mm Group. Communication between the two stations is by bell codes as in prototype signalling

Newport (Gwent) MRC's 'Long Suffren' layout is of the continuous-run type with a scenic station area on one side and storage sidings on the other. The aim is to present the viewer with a varied sequence of trains passing through the station

A 'Sentinel' steam railcar coals-up for the day on the Oxford MRC's 'Winton' layout. These cars were once extensively used by the LNER and make a popular prototype for modellers. Note how careful placing of accessories and figures has produced a scene with real atmosphere

'playing trains' and the smooth, fuss-free displays put on by teams who really know their layouts and have thoroughly rehearsed their programmes.

While the layout was still in the design stage you should have formed a pretty good idea of how it would be worked, what sort of traffic pattern there would be, and what part you most want to play: driver, signalman, traffic manager or CME.

Most layouts are worked to some sort of timetable. This can be either 'station based' in which the viewer/operator follows the progress of a typical day at a single station on the line, watching trains come and go: the morning and evening commuter peaks, the long-distance trains in the middle of the day, and the fast goods and ballast trains at night, with the odd pick-up goods threading their way through available 'paths' in the pattern; or it can be 'train based', in which the operator follows the progress of a single train from start to stop. In case the reader should think this is a bit like 'tail chasing' I can only say that one of the most entertaining layouts I know is worked on this system, and takes real skill to operate successfully.

The short distances involved in models and the limited time available for working them make the use of real time rather cumbersome. Many modellers use 'fast clocks' which have had parts of their gearing or escapements altered so as to make them run several times faster than normal; thus a full day's timetable might be run through in a couple of hours or less. While a very fast clock can be used for timing main-line movements, it is impossible to shunt realistically at much more than normal speed, and ample time should be allowed for any station moves involving shunting. One solution is to have a multi-speed clock which can be slowed down to 'real time' for station stops.

It is difficult for one person to control more than one train at a time, so a large layout, where several stations and the services between them are all worked to timetable, will need a number of operators. Such layouts are mostly owned by clubs, but some are run by small groups of friends who meet at regular intervals for a 'running night', and there is great satisfaction to be had from taking part in a group operation of this kind. At the same time, a domestic layout should be planned so that the owner can operate at least part of it single-handed.

Timetable operation need not be repetitive. Although nowadays goods traffic is largely concerned with block loads between main cities, a feature of the steam era was the 'pick-up goods' which ambled from station to station on a fairly leisurely schedule, setting out and picking up wagons as the day-to-day traffic required. Thus, although the train ran at roughly the same time each day, its make-up and the activity at the various stations would hardly ever repeat themselves exactly. Reproducing this operation in model form can be quite fascinating, especially if some random method is used to determine the pick-ups and set-outs on any given run. For example, you could make up two packs of cards, one representing all your wagons and the other all the possible goods transfer points (goods sheds, factory sidings, coal staithes and so on) on the layout. Shuffle the two packs independently, then take the top card from each pack; they might read 'Ventilated van — Bloggs' Brewery siding'. Repeat this say, ten times and you have a list of the vehicles to be set down. A further pack could determine which of the vehicles already at the various sidings were to be picked up. Making up the initial train, shunting it at each station with due attention to the times at which the main line must be left clear for other trains, and finally bringing it to its destination on time, will probably occupy an entire evening — with the certainty that the pattern will be quite different next time. Other 'games of chance' can be devised involving cards, dice, tops and so on.

The 'Hazard Pack' can also be quite useful in giving variety to a fairly stereotyped schedule. At intervals — which might be one scale hour — the operator takes a card from the pack. Many will be blank, but some will carry instructions such as '12.30 ex Bristol 35 mins late due to trackwork delay at Taunton' or '2.05 Birmingham to run in two portions with 15 min interval'. To cope with these out-of-the-ordinary situations, finding alternative coaches for the return service or rescheduling it, arranging platform allocations and stock for 'extras' and so on, and at the same time keeping the ordinary timetable going in orderly fashion, is a real test of one's organising and operating skill; a layout run on these lines can never become dull.

Sooner or later you may want to exhibit your layout at a local show. Exhibiting is a special skill; the public pay to see trains running, and you should try to arrange the working programme so that there is nearly always something to be seen moving. To give a successful show requires locos, track and rolling stock which perform faultlessly; operators who know the layout intimately and can cope with minor upsets without panicking or losing their tempers; and good planning. Practise transporting the layout and setting it up again; note the time taken and what goes wrong. Work out a programme in detail and stick to it (no need for a 'hazard pack' here!). Make sure the organisers of the show have arranged for adequate access to the hall for setting-up, out-of-hours maintenance (if the show lasts more than one day) and dismantling. Do a few shows as an assistant on someone else's layout before trying it with your own. Exhibition running is quite hard work but immensely satisfying when you have done your homework and everything goes right.

MAINTENANCE

A model railway which does not work gives very little satisfaction either to its owner or the spectator. All working mechanisms require a certain amount of effort, first to get them into first-class working order and then to keep them so. The maintenance of a model railway resolves itself into three major areas; damage repairs, lubrication and track cleaning.

Damage repairs should be very infrequent if the layout is properly built and operated in a sensible way so that derailments are rare. However, under this heading we can also consider replacement of wearing parts such as motors, wheels and bearings. The modern 00 gauge mechanism is made to stand hard work, and on most layouts will run for many years with only routine cleaning, but on layouts for exhibition use, or where a 'train based' timetable system is in operation, the axle bearings should be of extra generous size, and extra care should be taken in assembling the motion so as to obtain free running with a minimum of 'slop'. The Triang X04 motor has been known to last for more than 100 real miles' running, and a chassis to match this is not hard to build. Generally wear is reduced by making the parts of different metals, eg; steel axles in bronze bushes.

The standard motto for lubrication is 'little and often' and this is equally true of model railway equipment. Large quantities of oil can do no good, since the excess does not reach the rubbing surfaces, but simply spreads all over the vehicle, attracting dirt and spoiling the paintwork. Most bearings on a model loco require no more than one small drop at a time; this can be applied on the end of a thin wire or with a hypodermic needle. Oil for model use should not be too thin; '3 in 1' is often used, but SAE 20W-50 motor oil is better. Fast-running gears in particular throw thin oil off very quickly; molybdenum-disulphide grease, which you can buy from a garage, is better for these. Some oils attack plastics, so if in doubt do a test on a piece of scrap material first. Plastic-in-plastic bearings, as found on some Airfix kits and N gauge vehicles, can be lubricated with graphite powder or soft pencil lead. In particular, do not over-oil motors; excess oil can soften the brushes and cause shorting or sparking.

Some of the aerosol-packed cleaning fluids can be quite useful to the modeller. Radiospares electrical cleaning fluid is exceptionally good, as it does not leave a deposit or attack normal model paints; you can get it from a radio dealer. Apart from cleaning track, it can also be used for washing old oil and grease out of loco mechanisms during a major overhaul. Radiospares also supply a switch cleaner which contains a certain amount of lubricant; another popular cleaner which contains both lubricant and a rust inhibitor is WD-40, obtainable from car accessory shops. These cannot be used near scenery because of the oily deposit they leave.

The biggest single cause of unreliability in small model railways is poor wheel-to-rail contact caused by dirt. We have already seen (Chapter 6) how this can be alleviated by proper design, but all locos will run better on clean track and with clean wheels. Abrasive cleaners are sold for track-cleaning, but they generate a great deal of loose dirt which very quickly finds its way back on to the wheels. Nothing more than RS cleaning fluid or lighter fuel on a clean cotton rag should be necessary; if an abrasive cleaner is used to shift a particularly stubborn patch, the track should be cleaned with cleaning fluid and rag afterwards. Running an intensive train service helps to keep plain track clean but makes pointwork dirty.

Locomotive wheels tend to collect a coating of 'mud' consisting of powdered metal from the rails. This can be removed by running the loco upside-down and holding a brass wire brush against the wheels. You can get brushes which have two tufts of brass wire connected to wires with crocodile-clips for connecting to the power pack, so that the current is supplied through the pair of wheels being cleaned; this also shows up any faulty collectors, which can be cleaned and adjusted at the same time. Bogie and tender wheels can best be cleaned with a small rotary brass wire brush in a mini-drill; hold the brush at a slight angle and 'brake' the opposite wheel lightly with a finger to ensure a good scrubbing action. Wheels that have been cleaned in this way should be wiped over with cleaning fluid afterwards to remove loose dirt and dust.

Now and again, blow or brush the carbon dust away from the

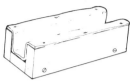

Cradle for loco maintenance

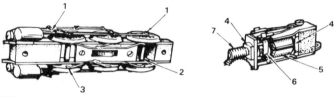

Maintenance points on a loco mechanism

1   One small drop of oil on each motion joint, including piston rod and slide bars.
2   Main axle bearings: one drop of oil each.
3   Collectors (if fitted): remove dirt and fluff and check adjustment.
4   Motor oil felts: 2 - 3 drops oil on each.
5   Magnet gaps: check for foreign matter and remove with paper feelers and sticky tape (do not dismantle motor).
6   Brushes: check for wear. Clean commutator only if necessary.
7   Worm and wormwheel: lubricate with thick oil or molybdenum disulphide grease

LOCO: 0-6-0 PT. 5747

DATE	FAULT	REPTD. BY	DATE	FAULT FOUND / ACTION	BY
3/11/76	Jerky running	BJt.	4/11/76	Wheels dirty. Cleaned.	BT
6/11/76	Derailed on up station crossover.	AW.	8/11/76	Fault would not repeat. Probably due to dirt in switch – see entries under 2884 & 4819 same date.	SHf
20/11/76	Noisy.	MG.	20/11/76	Mech. dry. Oiled all bearings.	MG

Typical fault log page

commutator end of the motor, check the brushes for wear and see if the commutator is clean. If it needs cleaning, do this with the end of a matchstick or a bit of balsawood strip dipped in lighter fuel or cleaning fluid. Do not use abrasive unless the commutator is pitted by sparking, and then use only 'flour' grade sandpaper. If a motor regularly pits its commutator it probably has a faulty winding or very weak brush springs.

A wooden cradle lined with soft cloth or chamois leather is useful to hold locos upside-down for cleaning without damaging fine detail.

All maintenance involves the risk of creating new faults, so test each loco carefully after cleaning and oiling. Even if the layout proper is run with transistor controllers, it is a good idea to keep a simple resistance controller available for testing; it may reveal faults which the more sophisticated controller can cover up. Current consumption is a good guide to a loco's condition; an increase from normal indicates stiffness or possibly a damaged magnet, while an intermittent drop indicates the need for commutator or wheel cleaning.

Many otherwise expert modellers seem to believe that derailments are unavoidable. *This is not true.* If you adopt a sufficiently ruthless attitude they can be virtually eliminated. The thing _not_ to do, when a derailment occurs, is simply to re-rail the stock and press on. On a full-size railway both the track and vehicles involved in a derailment are immediately taken out of service until an inquiry has established the cause and something has been done about it. Every model railway should have a track gauge and a back-to-back gauge; application of these to the track and to each pair of wheels in the derailed stock should establish which is at fault, and the item can then be rectified at once or logged for urgent attention.

Where a layout is run by a large number of operators, it may not be possible to pass on all 'accident reports' verbally and a fault log is used. This consists simply of a notebook, preferably loose-leaf, in which a note is made of each malfunction, what was found to be wrong and what was done to put it right. Columns can be provided for dates, times and signatures if necessary. If each loco and vehicle is given its own page or pages, it soon becomes apparent which ones are experiencing most troubles and these can be given special attention.

Some modellers also like to keep 'vehicle history logs' recording dates of building, repairs and modifications plus any special notes on the construction.

THE MODELLER'S WORKSHOP

Although some people can turn out superb models under the most adverse circumstances, it is much easier if you have good tools and good working conditions. It is difficult to do good work if you cannot see what you are doing or are uncomfortable, so good light and warmth are high on the list of priorities.

If the whole of one room is given over to the railway, it should be easy to fit a workbench. An old kitchen cabinet or chest of drawers, provided with a chipboard top covered with lino, can make an excellent bench; or you can build your own. The essential thing is that it must be steady; it is almost impossible to do accurate work on a bench that wobbles.

Much modelling work can be done in the living-room without creating an unacceptable mess, and many people — even if they have a workshop as well — like to do this to avoid the charge of neglecting their families for their hobby. A sheet of blockboard about 18in x 24in will protect the table; a sheet of baize or rubber mat can be stuck to one side for better protection. With such a work-top and a box of simple tools, a lot of kit assembly and similar small jobs can be done while the rest of the family watches television.

A development of this approach is the 'desk workshop' where a bureau or roll-top desk is used as a workbench when open and provides storage for tools and work in progress when closed. Some really well-equipped workshops, even incorporating small lathes such as the Unimat or Adept, have been assembled in this way.

Even if the model railway itself is all 'out of the box' some tools will still be necessary for building the basic structure; these will generally be the normal household handyman's kit of saw, hammer, screwdrivers, Surform and perhaps a chisel or two.

Plastic and white-metal kits can usually be assembled with no more than a razor saw and a few small files, and the card, wood or plastic parts of scratch-built rolling stock and buildings can be made with these plus a craft knife, steel rule and set-square. Once we start to make our own parts in metal, however, it becomes essential to be able to hold them still, and a good vice is a vital

A firm, smooth working surface well lit, and tools and materials ready to hand — the basics of an efficient workshop

part of the modeller's armoury. A small one which clamps on the corner of the table or the work-top is better than nothing, but if a permanent bench is installed, get a proper engineer's vice with about 4in jaws and bolt it solidly in place. Most vices have serrated jaws and loose smooth liners which are attached as required; for model work this situation must be reversed, the permanent jaws being 'blind' and toothed ones only being used on the rare occasions when they are necessary. Sometimes the conversion is simply a matter of turning the jaw liners round; if not, your tool merchant can supply 'ground flat stock' from which new liners can be cut. It is well worth taking a bit of trouble to set up the liners so that they close really square, parallel and flat and level on top. After a lot of use the flat surfaces will become worn and inaccurate; the liners can be turned over, reground or replaced. A small milling vice is useful, as are toolmakers' clamps and pin tongs for holding small jobs in the hand.

The really essential tool for the modeller in metal is the piercing saw. This is like a fretsaw but has a shorter, stiffer frame and takes hardened blades ranging from the M5 with 32 teeth per inch to the M4/0 which has 80 teeth per inch and is only .006in thick. Although fine, these blades are quite strong; they are placed in the frame with the teeth pointing towards the handle and thus cut on the 'pull' stroke.

The following hand tools can be obtained as and when required and will make up a fairly comprehensive modeller's tool kit.

Needle files: flat, round, half-round, knife, square, 3-square, 8in smooth flat file for truing long edges.

Pliers (various shapes) and tweezers. Get the best you can afford: bad ones will 'spit' small parts into limbo and waste a lot of your time.

Tin snips, wire cutters: again get the best you can afford.

Twist drills (see accompanying table) and a hand brace. Pin chuck to hold the smallest ones.

Scriber, steel rule, square and centre punch for marking out.

Hammers: 2oz and 4oz ball pein. Pin punch.

Both hard and soft soldering are easily learnt and essential to the complete modeller. In all cases the essentials are cleanliness and adequate heat. Most 00 gauge soldering requires a mains-powered iron of at least 25-watt rating. Many small irons, designed for electronic wiring, run too cool for model work. (Ask the dealer which sort *he* uses). An old-fashioned 'common bit' of about 8oz that can be heated up on a gas stove is a useful back-up for large jobs. Practise soldering with both solder paint ('Fryolux') and resin-cored solder until you can confidently make a sound, well-wetted joint every time. If the solder does not run within a couple of seconds of applying the bit to the work, it is either not big enough or not hot enough.

For Gauges 0 and 1 you will almost certainly need silver soldering; this is just as easy but involves getting the job red-hot with a gas-air torch. There are several which run on canned butane, but if you are going to do a lot of hard soldering it is better to get a propane torch such as those made by Primus-Sievert. A few firebricks will make a 'hearth' suitable for most small work.

The mention of machine tools often frightens the newcomer — but the hand-brace is a simple machine tool, and most of us have one of those! A small pillar drill makes hole-drilling much more accurate; a lathe makes possible all kinds of modelling jobs which

Turning a taper boiler for a 2mm scale locomotive out of solid brass rod. This is more commonly done in the very small scales; in 00 and larger the boiler is usually rolled up from sheet

Drilling the crankpin hole in a driving wheel, using a simple jig to ensure that the 'throw' on all wheels is the same

Principles of micrometer (above) and vernier caliper.

In the micrometer the thimble has just uncovered the third small division past 0.2 in; making 0.275 in; plus 8 divisions on the thimble 0.008 in; making 0.283 in altogether.

In the vernier the index is past the 0.3 in mark, and the 17th division of the vernier scale is in line with a mark on the main scale, making a total of 0.317 in.

Some useful twist drill sizes

Inch	BS No.	Metric equivalent	Remarks
.020	76	0.5	Common pin sizes
.024	73	0.6	
1/32		0.8	
.036	64	0.9	Common size for N/2mm axles
.041	59	1.05	12 BA tapping; running fit for 1mm
3/64		1.25	Running fit for 18 SWG; reaming size for .050in.
.052	55	1.4	12 BA clear; 10 BA tapping
.059	53	1.5	Running fit 1.5mm (N driving axles); reaming size 1/16in.
.070	50	1.75	00 axles; 10 BA clear; 8 BA tap
.089	43	2.25	8 BA clear; 6 BA tap, reaming size for 3/32in.
.113	33	2.9	6 BA clear; 4 BA tapping
.120	31	3.1	Reaming size for 1/8in. (00 driving axles)
.152	24	3.9	4 BA clear
3/16		4.75	

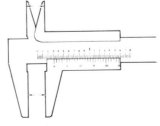

one could not tackle by hand. Get the lathe first, and if you can afford it and have enough space, get a fairly big one such as a Myford ML10; not only will it last longer and be more versatile, but you can then use it to machine castings to make up other machine tools, such as the pillar drill or a milling machine. Many small milling jobs can be done on the lathe itself with an attachment. A good second-hand lathe is a better bet for the newcomer than a brand-new one. By all means be careful when using machine tools; but do not be afraid of them — they are there to serve you.

Similarly a lot of people are needlessly put off by the idea of precise measurement. In certain areas — loco chimneys, for instance — quite tiny differences in size can make all the difference between the model that looks like a model and one that looks like the real thing. The most versatile measuring tool is the vernier caliper — you can get a good Japanese one for about £5, and it will measure in inches or millimetres to an accuracy of about .001in. You can also use it to convert between inch and metric dimensions. A micrometer is easier to use and slightly more accurate, but less versatile.

There are some other tools you will need, but these cannot be bought in a shop. They are an observant eye, an inquiring mind, and a determination that each model shall be a little bit better than the last one. Very few of us are born without the basic seeds of these things, but it is up to us to cultivate and develop them. If this book has brought any of its readers nearer to owning this part of the tool-kit, the time it took to write will have been very well spent.

INDEX